UNOFFICIAL
STEM QUEST
for MINECRAFTERS

GRADES 1–2

Stephanie J. Morris

Illustrated by Amanda Brack

SKY PONY PRESS
NEW YORK, NY

Copyright © 2019 by Hollan Publishing, Inc.

Minecraft® is a registered trademark of Notch Development AB.
The Minecraft game is copyright © Mojang AB.

Sky Pony Press books may be purchased in bulk at special
discounts for sales promotion, corporate gifts, fund-raising, or
educational purposes. Special editions can also be created to
specifications. For details, contact the Special Sales Department,
Sky Pony Press, 307 West 36th Street, 11th Floor, New York, NY
10018 or info@skyhorsepublishing.com.

Sky Pony® is a registered trademark of Skyhorse Publishing, Inc.®,
a Delaware corporation.

Visit our website at www.skyponypress.com.

Authors, books, and more at SkyPonyPressBlog.com.

10 9 8 7 6 5 4 3 2 1

Library of Congress Cataloging-in-Publication Data is available on file.

Cover design by Brian Peterson

Photos (including cover art) by Stephanie J. Morris, except pages
13, 15, 25, 35 (bag), 47, and 56 by Shutterstock

Illustrations by Amanda Brack, except pages 6, 27 (numbers), 36-
37 (snowflakes), and 51 by Shutterstock

Interior design by Joanna Williams
Interior art by Amanda Brack

Print ISBN: 978-1-5107-4113-3

Printed in China

A NOTE TO PARENTS

What if kids could take the skills and concepts used in Minecraft and apply them to **REAL-WORLD EXPLORATION**? Minecraft could become an inspirational tool, and the child could become the investigator. What an adventure!

Minecraft is an amazing game that allows children to explore new concepts in a controlled environment. The game is based on the premise of extracting resources from their environment to build and create structures of their own. Crafters are learning about natural resources, ecosystem relationships, physics, math, architecture, engineering, and so much more. In short, they are learning STEM.

STEM Quest for Minecrafters is an engaging collection of STEM experiments which will allow early elementary school–age children to **EXPLORE AND PROBLEM SOLVE** at home. Minecrafters will have the time of their lives conducting incredibly fun and creative experiments using simple, easy-to-find materials. Children will explore the properties of motion, chemical changes, earth science, chromatography, engineering, binary codes, botany, computer graphics, and many other real-world concepts.

Engage in these activities with your child. Experience new discoveries together. Encourage kids to **DEVELOP THEIR CURIOSITY** while exploring the natural world.

While all of these projects are kid-friendly and encourage little ones to get involved, some of the experiments require or strongly benefit from parental supervision. Look for the redstone dust icon to know when help or extra caution is needed.

CONTENTS

POPPING TNT

Create an explosive chemical reaction with expanding gases.

You may have used **BAKING SODA** and **VINEGAR** to make "lava" bubble out of a model volcano, but now you can use those same ingredients to create an **EXPLOSION**. Here, you will have to act quickly and get out of the way before your TNT bag's chemical reactions make a big mess of things. This is the perfect outdoor **STEM** project for curious Minecrafters.

INSTRUCTIONS

1. Write "TNT" on the zipper-seal bag with a permanent marker.

2. Line a table with wax paper. Open a facial tissue (if it is two-ply, only use one layer) and lay it flat on the wax paper. In the center, place 3 tablespoons of baking soda. Add 10–12 drops of yellow food coloring to the baking soda. Carefully fold the tissue around the baking soda to make a packet. Set the baking soda packet aside.

3. Carefully pour the vinegar into the zipper-seal bag.

4. Add 4–6 drops of red food coloring to the vinegar.

5. Add a generous squirt of dish soap to the vinegar.

6. Take your project outside.

7. Zip the bag partway closed.

8. Place the tissue paper with the baking soda in the bag of vinegar.

9. Quickly zip the bag completely closed.

10. Move away from the bag and observe.

WHAT REALLY HAPPENED?

✳ Hopefully, your TNT bag bubbled, expanded, and then popped. Pretty cool! Inside the bag, the baking soda and vinegar mixed to create an acid-base reaction. In the process, the two chemicals created the gas carbon dioxide.

✳ Gas needs room to expand, so carbon dioxide filled the bag until the bag could not hold any more gas. As a result, the bag popped.

TIME
10 minutes

MATERIALS

- ◆ black permanent marker
- ◆ zipper-seal freezer bag (quart)
- ◆ 1 tissue
- ◆ wax paper
- ◆ 3 tbsp baking soda
- ◆ 1 cup vinegar
- ◆ dish soap (Dawn)
- ◆ 10–12 drops yellow food coloring
- ◆ 4–6 drops red food coloring

YOUR TURN TO EXPERIMENT

Think of ways you could change the experiment. What would happen if you changed the size of the bag, the temperature of the vinegar, or the amount of baking soda? **MAKE ONE OF THESE CHANGES AND RECORD YOUR OBSERVATIONS BELOW.**

OBSERVATIONS:

FREE-FLOATING GHAST

Use static to make an object move.

Don't be shocked by this hair-raising experiment! **STATIC ELECTRICITY** makes objects stick together by creating **OPPOSITE CHARGES**. In this activity, you'll make a tissue-paper ghast that can float. All you have to do is use a balloon to harness the power of static electricity.

INSTRUCTIONS

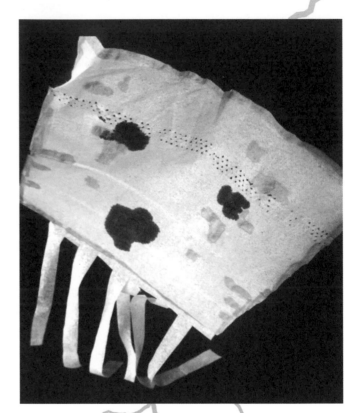

1. Cut a ghast shape out of the tissue. Feel free to add details like eyes, a mouth, and long legs.

2. If you are using tissues, carefully pull the two layers of tissue apart so that you just have one layer—now you have 2 ghasts!

3. Blow up the balloon and tie the end.

4. Rub the balloon very quickly through your hair for at least 10 seconds. (Or you can rub the balloon on a piece of wool fabric.) This adds static charge.

5. Slowly bring the charged balloon near the ghast. The ghast will start to rise up toward the balloon, and it might even try to attach itself to the balloon.

6. Practice with the balloon and the ghast. You might get good enough to have the ghast float over the surface of the table.

MATERIALS

- tissue or tissue paper
- scissors
- balloon
- your head (or a piece of wool fabric)

WHAT REALLY HAPPENED?

※ Rubbing a balloon on your head created static electricity. Static electricity is the buildup of electrical charge in an object. Static electricity causes objects to stick together, like when a sock sticks to a fuzzy sweater in the laundry. This happens when objects have opposite charges (positive and negative) that attract.

※ When you rubbed the balloon on your head, you created a charge on the balloon. When you brought the charged balloon close to the lightweight tissue, the tissue was attracted to the balloon. This caused the tissue to move toward the balloon.

YOUR TURN TO EXPERIMENT

Make floating ghasts out of different types of paper— facial tissues, bathroom tissues, tissue paper, or white paper are options to consider. **WHICH TYPE OF PAPER WAS EASIEST TO CONTROL?**

OBSERVATIONS:

I ♥ PIXELS

Use coordinates to draw like a computer.

When you open Minecraft on a computer, you can see all of your favorite characters on the screen. Whether it's a creeper, a zombie, or a witch, your computer needs **NUMBER INFORMATION** to know how to draw these mobs on the screen. In this activity, you will learn how computers use **COORDINATES** (numbers that give a location) to make those pictures.

INSTRUCTIONS:

Coordinates are numbers on a grid that give a location. In the case of a computer graphics coordinate system, the first number tells the computer how many location steps across, and the second number tells the computer how many steps down.

For example, if you wanted to put a red dot in the middle of the graph on the right, you would give the computer these coordinates:

(3, 3 red)

The first number tells the computer to go 3 pixels to the right (starting at the upper left-hand corner of the screen).

The second number tells the computer to drop 3 squares down. The word red tells the computer to fill in that pixel with the color red.

0	1	2	3	4	5
1					
2					
3					
4					
5					

Now *you* be the computer. Use the coordinates below to draw a smiley face on the screen at right. The first pixel is drawn for you: 2 to the right, 2 down, black.

See if you can use the coordinates to draw the rest.

~~(2, 2 black)~~ ■   (6, 4 black) ■   (3, 6 black) ■
(5, 2 black) ■   (2, 5 black) ■   (4, 6 black) ■
(1, 4 black) ■   (5, 5 black) ■

0	1	2	3	4	5	6
1						
2		■				
3						
4						
5						
6						

YOUR TURN TO EXPERIMENT

❋ Use graph paper to represent your computer screen (or use a white piece of paper to trace the grid shown above). Number the grid as shown and shade in the eyes and mouth of a creeper face.

❋ Write the coordinates for the pixels you colored in. Have a friend or family member be the computer and try to draw a creeper face on a new paper using only your coordinates. Did it work?

PIXEL POWER

Computers draw images using pixels, which are tiny points of color. Pixels make up the images you see on computer games like Minecraft. Minecraft uses thousands of images with very noticeable pixels.

EFFERVESCING POTION

Make a bubbling chemical reaction in a bottle.

Potions in Minecraft have lots of uses. They can help you in combat by giving you strength, healing, or swiftness. This potion isn't safe to drink, but it's a lot of fun to make and watch. You'll use Alka-Seltzer tablets to **CREATE BUBBLES OF CARBON DIOXIDE** that make the potion move and dance. If this were a potion, it would be called the potion of Knowledge.

INSTRUCTIONS

1. Measure 2 cups of vegetable oil and pour into your glass jar or bottle.

2. Add 1 cup of water. Record your observation in the table below.

3. Add 5–6 drops of food coloring.

4. Place your jar over a pie tin or cookie sheet.

5. Remove one Alka-Seltzer tablet from the wrapper and break into 4 pieces.

6. Add one piece of the Alka-Seltzer tablet at a time and enjoy the show! Record your observations in the table below.

7. You can continue adding Alka-Seltzer tablets to continue the reaction.

 Remind kids that this potion is not safe for drinking.

WHAT REALLY HAPPENED?

❋ You may have heard the phrase "oil and water do not mix." This is why: when water is added to oil, it sinks to the bottom and the oil floats to the top. Oil floats because it is less dense (the molecules are packed more loosely) than the water.

❋ Adding Alka-Seltzer to oil and water started a chemical reaction. The Alka-Seltzer reacted with water to form carbon dioxide gas. The gas attached itself to a few water molecules, and together the water molecules and carbon dioxide made bubbles that floated to the surface. When it reached the surface of the "potion," the bubbles popped and released the carbon dioxide into the air. Then, the water molecules (now empty bubbles) returned to the bottom of the jar.

MATERIALS

- 2 cups vegetable oil
- glass jar or bottle (large enough to contain 3 cups of liquid, plus space for bubbling)
- 1 cup water
- 5-6 drops food coloring
- pie tin or cookie sheet for containing spills
- 1 box of Alka-Seltzer tablets

YOUR TURN TO EXPERIMENT

❄ Try adding a few drops of a different food coloring. What happens?

❄ Time the reaction from when you place the Alka-Seltzer tablet in the oil-water mixture to when the bubbles form and move. How long does it take? How long does it last?

❄ How could Steve or Alex use a bubbling potion like this one in the game of Minecraft? What effect would it have? Would it make a player fly? Would it make creepers stop exploding? **USE THE SPACE BELOW TO EXPLAIN.**

CRYSTALLINE DIAMONDS

Witness the process of nucleation.

Diamonds are an **IMPORTANT RESOURCE** in Minecraft. They can be used to make armor, weapons, and beacons. In the real world, **CRYSTALS** are used to make watches, tools, and even surgery scalpels! Learn how to make your own spectacular **CRYSTALLINE DIAMONDS** in this experiment that allows you to observe over time.

INSTRUCTIONS

1. Choose a chenille wire and food coloring to match the color of crystal you would like to make.

2. Twist 2–3 inches of the chenille wires into a shape (sphere, cube, teardrop).

3. Tie one end of the thread around the chenille wire.

4. Attach the chenille wire to the skewer using the thread. The shape needs to hang into the pot so that it is submerged but not touching the bottom of the pot. Set the skewer with the chenille wire hanging down into the empty pot. After you are satisfied with the length of the thread, remove the skewer and chenille wire and set aside.

5. Fill the pot with water and add the food coloring.

6. With the help of a grown-up, bring the colored water to a simmer and add Borax powder until the solution is supersaturated. You will know that you have a supersaturated solution when a little Borax remains at the bottom of the pot. At this point, you can turn off the stove.

7. Lay the skewer across the top of the pot with the chenille wire hanging down into the Borax solution.

8. Cover the pot with the lid, then use aluminum foil to seal in the heat. Layer towels over the top of the pot to keep the heat in the pot as long as possible.

9. Wait 24 hours until the pot has completely cooled before removing the crystal formation.

MATERIALS

- chenille wires
  (2–3 inches)
- thread
  (about 3–4 inches)
- skewer
- large pot with lid
- water
- food coloring
- Borax
- aluminum foil
- towels

WHAT REALLY HAPPENED?

❋ Crystals start growing by a process called nucleation. The particles in the solution (Borax in this activity) are attracted to each other and form bonds. The particles naturally arrange in a regular and repeated pattern to form a solid called a crystal.

YOUR TURN TO EXPERIMENT

❋ Make a variety of different crystals.
Try growing different colors of crystals or use other substances, such as sugar, salt, alum, or Epsom salts to create them.

❋ Consider waiting longer than 24 hours to pull your crystals out of the solution next time. What happens to the size of the crystal if you wait?

Note to parents: *To return your crystal pot to normal, simply fill with water and return it to the stove on medium low. After everything has turned back to a liquid, you can pour the contents down the drain.*

MINIATURE BOW-AND-ARROW

Watch physics in action.

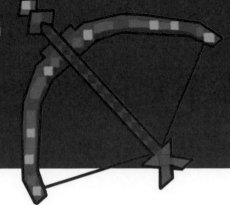

Bow and arrows are handy weapons for defeating creepers and skeletons from a safe distance, but have you ever thought about how they work? This experiment lets you create your own working bow-and-arrow so you can see **ENERGY TRANSFER** and **TRAJECTORIES** in action.

INSTRUCTIONS

1. Have an adult use the glue gun to place a drop of hot glue in the opening of 1 wooden cube.

2. Push a dowel rod through the glue and into the hole until it is flush with the other side of the cube. This will be the front of your bow.

3. Repeat Step 1 with a second cube and add the new cube to the other end of the dowel rod.

4. Have an adult glue a stepped row of three additional cubes to one side of a cube attached to the dowel rod (see photo). Make sure the holes face the same direction as those of the first cube. Repeat this process on the other side of the dowel rod to create the frame of your bow.

5. Cut the rubber band.

6. After the glue has dried and hardened on the frame, insert one end of the rubber band through the last cube you attached. Then insert it through a bead.

7. Tie the end of the rubber band to keep it from sliding back through the bead.

8. Repeat Steps 6–7 for the other side of the bow.

9. Use the remaining dowel rods as arrows. Grip the dowel rod with one hand and pull the arrow back (pinching it against the rubber band). Release and let the arrow soar!

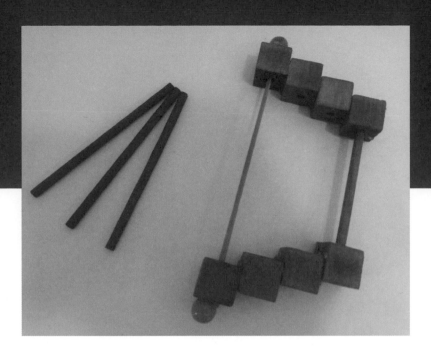

TIME

15–20 minutes

MATERIALS

◆ glue gun and hot glue sticks

◆ 8 miniature wooden cubes with center holes (available at most craft stores with dowel rods included)

◆ 2–4 small dowel rods

◆ rubber band

◆ 2 small beads

WHAT REALLY HAPPENED?

※ When you pulled back on the bowstring, you used your muscles to exert a force on the string. When you let go, your energy was transferred to the rubber band, which used the energy to launch the arrow forward. The more you pull back on the bowstring, the more energy is transferred, which makes the arrow fly farther.

※ When an arrow is released, it follows an arch-shaped path, called a trajectory. When you shoot it, the arrow is catapulted forward and upward. As it loses energy, gravity pulls the arrow back toward the Earth.

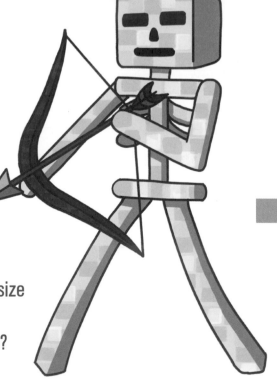

YOUR TURN TO EXPERIMENT

※ Try changing the sizes of the bow and arrows. What size combination shoots the arrows the longest distance? What other household objects can you use as arrows? How about cotton-tipped swabs?

NEWTON'S FLYING BAT

Create a bat that flies using Newton's Third Law of Motion.

Explore a cave in Minecraft and, chances are, you'll see some bats hanging upside down or you'll hear them shrieking as they fly overhead. While creepy, these passive mobs won't hurt you. In this activity, they'll actually teach you a little about **PHYSICS**. Have fun making a Minecraft balloon bat that flies according to **NEWTON'S THIRD LAW OF MOTION**: For every action, there is an equal and opposite reaction.

INSTRUCTIONS

1. Using a marker, color the straw black. Allow it to dry. This is the bat's back.

2. Attach crepe paper "wings" to the center of the straw with glue dots.

3. Fold a piece of crepe paper into a rectangle to use as the bat's head. Glue small crepe paper ears and googly eyes to it to create the head.

4. Attach the head to the straw with glue dots.

5. Thread the fishing line (or dental floss) through the straw.

6. Tie the tail end of the fishing line onto a chair or other piece of furniture. Tie the other end, extending from the bat's head, to another higher piece of furniture.

7. Place two glue dots on the bat's belly area, near the center of the length of straw.

8. Inflate the balloon and pinch (do not tie) the end with your fingers or a clothespin to keep it inflated.

9. Attach the balloon to the glue dots on the bat's belly so the pinched end is pointing back behind the bat.

10. When you are ready, let go and watch your bat fly!

MATERIALS

- black permanent marker
- plastic straw
- black crepe paper
- glue dots
- scissors
- googly eyes
- 4–6 feet of fishing line or unwaxed dental floss
- 1 black balloon
- electrician's tape or black duct tape
- clothespin (optional)

WHAT REALLY HAPPENED?

☀ **ISAAC NEWTON** was a famous scientist. He was the first person to explain why objects drop when they are released in the air. He called the force that causes this gravity. He studied motion and wrote three very important laws or rules about it. This activity demonstrated Newton's Third Law of Motion, which explains that for every action, there is an equal and opposite reaction. When air traveled out of the balloon in one direction, it caused the balloon to move in the opposite direction.

YOUR TURN TO EXPERIMENT

☀ Have a bat-flying contest with a friend. Set up multiple zip lines for the bats and race to see whose bat is the fastest.

☀ Does the size of the balloon influence the distance that the bat travels? Try using larger and smaller balloons.

NETHER LAVA

Make bubbling lava to understand density and see how solids dissolve.

Turn your kitchen into the **NETHER** when you create jars of **OIL-AND-WATER LAVA** that bubbles just like the lava in your favorite game. Is it hot? No, but it's as close to real lava as you'll want to get, and it lets you watch what happens when a solid travels through liquids of **DIFFERENT DENSITIES**.

INSTRUCTIONS

1. Fill a clear jar or glass three-quarters full of water.

2. Add 5–10 drops of red food coloring.

3. Slowly pour the vegetable oil on top of the water.

4. Sprinkle some salt on top of the oil.

5. Carefully observe the lava float up and down in the water.

6. You can continue adding salt and keep watching.

WHAT REALLY HAPPENED?

❋ Oil floats because it is less dense than water.

❋ The salt is denser than the oil, so it sinks. When it passes through the layer of oil, some of the oil gets stuck to the salt. When the salt and oil reach the water, the salt dissolves in the water, and the oil floats back up to the surface.

MATERIALS

- clear jar or glass
- water
- red food coloring
- ¼ cup of vegetable oil
- salt (1 or more teaspoons)

YOUR TURN TO EXPERIMENT

Swap out the salt for other solid ingredients that dissolve easily, such as sugar or baking soda. What happens?

How long can you keep the reaction going by adding more salt? Chart your longest times here:

Amount of Salt	Reaction Time (in seconds)

SQUID CHROMATOGRAPHY
Find hidden colors in squid ink.

If you play Minecraft, you know that **SQUID** are passive mobs that drop ink sacs you can later use to create dyes. They use their tentacles to swim about, and they **RELEASE A CLOUD OF BLACK INK** to hide their escape when a player attacks. Real-life squid shoot black ink, too. If you could examine the ink more closely, you might find something surprisingly colorful. In this experiment, you'll use **CHROMATOGRAPHY** to see the **HIDDEN COLORS** that make up black ink.

INSTRUCTIONS

1. Cover your work surface with newspaper.

2. Using the marker, draw a black circle (a little bigger than the size of a quarter) in the center of the coffee filter and color it in darkly.

3. Place a cotton ball on top of the black circle.

4. Use the eyedropper to saturate the cotton ball with rubbing alcohol.

5. Secure the coffee filter around the cotton ball with the rubber band.

6. Cut into the coffee filter from the edges to give the squid eight legs.

7. Prop the squid up on its legs and watch! If nothing seems to be happening, you can add more rubbing alcohol to the top of the squid with the eyedropper.

8. Allow the ink to separate into various colors (the colors will differ depending upon the marker that is used) over the next 30–60 minutes.

TIME

30 minutes

MATERIALS

- newspaper
- fresh black washable marker
- paper coffee filter
- cotton ball
- eyedropper
- rubbing alcohol
- small rubber band (Rainbow Loom bands work well)
- scissors

WHAT REALLY HAPPENED?

✷ Chromatography is a process used to separate parts of a solution that has different chemicals inside it. Ink is made of several different molecules, each with their own size and color. What colors did you find in the ink you used?

✷ Each molecule in the ink travels at a different speed when pulled along the piece of paper. The most lightweight particles move more quickly and over greater distances than the heavier particles, kind of like a race.

YOUR TURN TO EXPERIMENT

Try making chromatograms using other colors of markers. What colors appear on the chromatograms?

SPIDER ENGINEERING
Build a spiderweb like an arachnid.

When spiders abandon their old webs, cobwebs linger in corners and near the ceiling, collecting dirt and dust. In Minecraft, these old webs slow things down. **SPIDERS ARE AMAZINGLY SKILLED ARCHITECTS**, making their webs with lots of details and artistic patterns. Do you have the skills necessary to build a web as beautiful as a real spider web?

INSTRUCTIONS

1. Find an image of a spiderweb online or find one in real life.

2. Tie one end of the dental floss to one branch of the stick.

3. Pretend you are a spider and weave a web that looks like the real thing. Move the floss in repeating patterns and cross over the center of your web again and again.

* Spiders spin webs to catch insects for food.

* The strongest silk is made by the golden orb spider. This spider's silk is stronger than steel, and fifty times lighter!

WHAT REALLY HAPPENED?

* Spiders make their webs out of silk, which is a special protein they produce. They make silk in a part of their body called a gland and use their legs to pull it out. This is called spinning.

REAL-LIFE CONNECTIONS

Go on a spiderweb hunt. Take a walk through the woods, carefully looking for spiderwebs. Draw any that you see here.

CRACK THE CODE

Use binary code to solve a riddle.

Binary code is how computers talk and represent information. **BINARY CODE is a TWO-NUMBER SYSTEM**, which means it uses only two numbers to make a code for all the information in a computer. Those numbers are 1 and 0. Everything you see on the computer (letters, numbers, and pictures) is made up of different **COMBINATIONS OF 1s AND 0s**. In this activity, you get to use computer code to solve a question!

INSTRUCTIONS

Take a look at the binary code alphabet below. It shows the computer code for each letter. This is how computers represent each letter of the alphabet. Use the chart to figure out the answer to the riddle.

A	01000001	N	01001110
B	01000010	O	01001111
C	01000011	P	01010000
D	01000100	Q	01010001
E	01000101	R	01010010
F	01000110	S	01010011
G	01000111	T	01010100
H	01001000	U	01010101
I	01001001	V	01010110
J	01001010	W	01010111
K	01001011	X	01011000
L	01001100	Y	01011001
M	01001101	Z	01011010

I TAKE JUST FOUR SECONDS TO EXPLODE WHEN ACTIVATED BY REDSTONE. WHAT AM I?

01010100	01001110	01010100

ACTIVATING END RODS
Discover how temperature affects glow sticks.

Travel bravely to the End and you'll probably notice **END RODS**, lighted sticks that naturally generate there. End rods are used in Minecraft for lighting and decoration, just like real-world glow sticks. Have you ever wondered why you need to **BEND A GLOW STICK** to make it light up? If so, prepare to be enLIGHTened.

INSTRUCTIONS

1. Before beginning this activity, feel the glow stick. How warm or cold does it feel? Write your observations on the chart.

2. Fill one glass cup with ice water.

3. Have a parent fill the second glass cup with very hot water (almost boiling).

4. Break one glow stick and observe the temperature again.

5. Break the second glow stick and shake both sticks to activate them completely.

6. At the same time, drop one glow stick into the ice water and one into the hot water.

7. Turn off the lights and watch. Jot down your observations on the chart below.

Observation Chart

Glow sticks before experiment	Glow sticks after breaking	Glow stick in ice water	Glow stick in hot water

MATERIALS

- 2 glow sticks of the same color
- 2 glass cups or jars
- ice water
- hot water

WHAT REALLY HAPPENED?

✻ When you bend the glow stick, a thin glass tube inside it breaks and releases a chemical. This chemical mixes with another chemical inside the larger plastic tube. When these two chemicals mix, light is produced. This is called **CHEMILUMINESCENCE.**

✻ Chemiluminescence does not produce any heat. You probably observed that the temperature of the glow stick was the same as the air around you and that its temperature did not change after it was activated.

✻ Chemical reactions happen at a faster rate with heat and are slowed down when cooled. The glow stick in the hot water should have glowed more brightly because the reaction was happening at a faster rate.

YOUR TURN TO EXPERIMENT

All glow sticks lose their glow after a few hours. Try putting one glow stick in the refrigerator or the freezer and the other glow stick in a warm place. Which glow stick stays bright the longest?

FLOWER PIGMENT POWER

Use natural pigments to make colorful art.

Young Minecrafters love using dyes to change the color of sheep in Minecraft. Gamers can also use Minecrafting resources like cocoa beans, cacti, and dandelions to **CREATE DYES** that change the color of armor, wolf collars, and shulkers. Nature provides an incredible variety of colors for us to use as pigments. Humans have used **PLANT PIGMENTS** for thousands of years to change the color of fabric, hair, and even skin. In this activity, you'll use the **FOOD AND PLANT RESOURCES** in your own kitchen and backyard to make fabric art.

INSTRUCTIONS

1. Cut the fabric to the desired size of the finished product. (If you plan to frame your cloth, allow space around the edge to wrap the fabric around the cardboard in the frame.)

2. Gather the plant products you intend to use as pigments. Cut the flowers from the stems. If using berries, smash them to release the juices.

3. Choose an area that can be safely pounded with a hammer. Sidewalks and driveways work well. If necessary, cover the work surface with newspaper to prevent staining.

4. Lay a piece of wax paper slightly larger than the cloth on the work surface. Then place the cloth on top.

5. When you are ready to begin, place flowers and leaves face down on the fabric. Add berry juices, coffee grounds, or vegetable parts in their desired locations.

6. Cover the fabric and plants with a second piece of wax paper.

7. Put on your eye protection. Carefully hammer the wax paper to transfer the plant pigments onto the fabric.

8. Remove the fabric and peel away the objects.

9. Rinse the fabric in cold water. Note: The pigments may fade after being washed.

WHAT REALLY HAPPENED

✺ Scientists believe that humans have been using plant pigments since the days of cave paintings way back in 15,000 BC. Egyptians dyed fibers starting in 2000 BC.

✺ Most plants contain a lot of different pigments. Pigments help plants stay alive and help us add color where we want it! The green pigment in a plant is called chlorophyll. It helps absorb energy from the sun to make food. Bright pigments in plants and fruit attract insects (like bees) that help plants reproduce.

YOUR TURN TO EXPERIMENT

Try dyeing different kinds of paper and fabric to see which one holds the color best. Make a chart to record what happens.

MATERIALS

◆ white or light-colored cotton fabric (for example, cloth napkins, rags, pillowcases)

◆ scissors

◆ plants and food items to use as pigments:

◆ coffee grounds

◆ fresh beets, thinly sliced—caution: may stain

◆ berries

◆ flower petals

◆ cabbage leaves

◆ tea bags

◆ wax paper

◆ eye protection

◆ hammer

STEM QUEST MATH MINUTE

Sharpen your math skills while you craft.

Numbers and adding are important in Minecraft when you need to gather enough ingredients in your inventory to make weapons, armor, food, tools, and much more. Use the **MINECRAFTING RECIPES** here to practice your math. Calculate the total number of items needed. Write your answers next to Items Total.

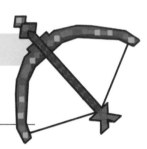

TNT

```
  5 gunpowder
+ 4 blocks of sand
_____
   items total
```

Bow

```
  3 sticks
+ 3 pieces of string
_____
   items total
```

Arrows

```
  1 stick
  1 feather
+ 1 flint
_____
   items total
```

Enchantment Table

```
  4 obsidian blocks
  2 diamonds
+ 1 book
_____
   items total
```

Wood Pickaxe

```
  2 sticks
+ 3 wood planks
_____
   items total
```

Bed

```
  3 blocks of wool
+ 3 planks
_____
   items total
```

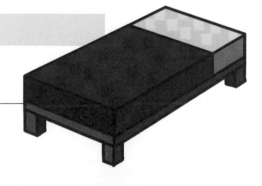

CRITICAL THINKING

Which ingredient is the most useful one based on
the recipes shown?

Which recipe requires the smallest number of items and the greatest
variety of items?

Write your own math formula for a new Minecraft weapon or tool below:

STORM MODELS

Recreate dramatic weather events

TIME
5–20 minutes for each part

MATERIALS (RAIN)

- glass jar or cup
- water
- white, foamy shaving cream
- 2–3 food coloring choices
- small bowls or cups
- 2–3 eyedroppers

The sky darkens, villagers return to their homes, and Endermen teleport away as it starts to pour. Storms occur in Minecraft with just as much intensity as they do in the real world. **MAKE MODELS** of rain, snow, and thunder in this activity and learn more about **METEOROLOGY**, the science of weather.

INSTRUCTIONS FOR THE RAIN MODEL

1. Fill a glass jar or cup with water, leaving 2–3 inches at the top for shaving cream.
2. Use shaving cream to make a cloud on top of the water.
3. In separate bowls or cups, mix water and food coloring.
4. Using a separate eyedropper for each color, squirt colored water on top of the shaving cream cloud. Repeat the process with the other colors in separate areas of the cloud.
5. Watch as the cloud gets heavy with water and precipitates colored rain.

WHAT REALLY HAPPENED?

Clouds form when water vapor rises into the air and condenses. When clouds become saturated with (full of) water, gravity pulls droplets toward the Earth, causing rain.

◆ 1 brown paper bag

INSTRUCTIONS FOR THE THUNDER MODEL

1. Blow into a brown paper lunch bag.

2. Twist the end of the bag closed.

3. Quickly hit the bag with your other hand.

WHAT REALLY HAPPENED

❋ When you hit the bag, the air inside the bag compressed quickly. This caused the bag to break when the air rushed out. As the air from inside the bag rushed out, it pushed the air outside the bag away. The movement of the air created a sound wave, which you heard as a bang.

❋ Thunder is created when lightning passes from a cloud to the Earth. As the lightning moves toward the Earth, it separates the air. After the lightning passes, the air collapses back together and creates a sound wave, which we hear as thunder.

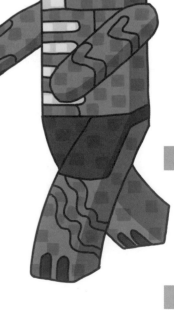

INSTRUCTIONS FOR THE SNOW MODEL

1. Place each diaper in the bowl and carefully cut the first layer of material. Remove the cotton from inside the diaper and set it aside.

2. Pour the powdery material from inside the diaper into the bowl. Repeat with the remaining diapers.

3. One ounce at a time, pour up to 4 ounces of water for each diaper used over the powder. Gently mix the powder and water with your fingers until it begins to thicken and form soft "snow."

4. Enjoy playing in the snow! How does this snow feel the same as or different from real snow?

MATERIALS (SNOW)

- 3-4 disposable baby diapers
- small bowl
- scissors
- 8-16 oz water

WHAT REALLY HAPPENED

❄ The tiny molecule chains that make up the material inside diapers expand when they are filled with water, just like sponges do. Some chains of molecules, called polymers, can soak up to 800 times their weight in water!

❄ Real snow forms when ice crystals in clouds stick together. When lots of ice crystals stick together, they become heavy enough to fall to the ground as snow.

SLIME FARM

Link molecules together to spawn your very own slimeballs!

Y ou have to battle lots of bouncing slimes to collect slimeballs when you're Minecrafting. Fortunately, you can make your own **STICKY** slimeballs in real life with no battles required. The key ingredients are white glue (a **POLYMER**) and a **SOLUTION** of sodium tetraborate decahydrate ($Na_2B_4O_7 \cdot 10H_2O$), called Borax.

◆ INSTRUCTIONS

1. Pour glue into a disposable cup.

2. Fill the glue bottle with warm water, replace the cap, and shake to mix.

3. Add the water from the glue bottle to the glue in the cup.

4. Use a craft stick to stir together.

5. Add 7–10 drops of green food coloring.

6. In a separate cup, dissolve the Borax in ½ cup of warm water and mix with the second craft stick until dissolved.

7. Slowly add the Borax and water mixture to the glue and water mixture, stirring as you pour.

8. Mix until combined and then use your hands to continue combining the slime. When you're done playing with your slime, store it in a bag.

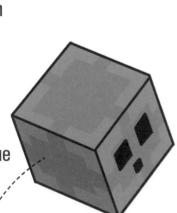

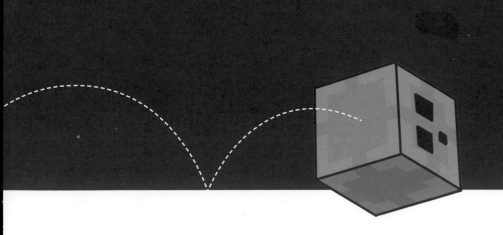

WHAT REALLY HAPPENED

Glue contains long flexible molecules called polymers. The polymers slide past each other in glue's liquid form. When the Borax solution (sodium tetraborate decahydrate, or $Na_2B_4O_7 \cdot 10H_2O$) is added to the glue, it links the glue polymers together. When they are linked together, they cannot slide around as easily. Adding the Borax changes the glue and water solution from a polymer to a new substance, which scientists and kids call slime!

YOUR TURN TO EXPERIMENT

What happens if you change the amount of Borax added to the glue solution?

Experiment with other types of glue, such as clear glue, glitter glue, or even glow-in-the-dark glue.

TIME

20 minutes

MATERIALS

- 4-oz. bottle of white school glue
- 2 disposable cups
- water
- 2 craft sticks
- green food coloring
- 1 teaspoon Borax
- ½ cup warm water
- zipper-seal sandwich bag to store the slime

COLOR-CREEPING CREEPER

Get an exciting look at capillary action.

Creepers are hostile mobs that sneak up on players, give off a short hissss, and then boom! **WATER** has special creeping abilities as well. Capillary action is water's superpower: it allows water to move in a way that **DEFIES GRAVITY.** Prepare to watch a creeper get its bright green color with the help of **CAPILLARY ACTION.**

INSTRUCTIONS

1. Fill the bowl with water and add several drops of green food coloring. Place it on a table lined with wax paper.

2. Cut the paper towel into a long, 2-inch strip.

3. Using the permanent marker, draw the outline of a creeper on one end of the paper towel strip.

4. Place the other end of the strip in the green water and extend the rest of the paper towel outside the bowl.

5. Let the creeping begin!

WHAT REALLY HAPPENED

※ In this activity, water moves through the paper towel by a process called capillary action. Water molecules are attracted to the paper towel, but they are also attracted to each other. As one water molecule travels up the paper towel, it grabs another water molecule to pull along. The process continues until the water reaches the end of the paper towel. How do you think this makes paper towels good for cleaning spills?

MATERIALS

- medium to large bowl (glass works best)
- water
- green food coloring
- wax paper
- scissors
- paper towels (two connected sheets)
- black permanent marker

❄ Plants use capillary action to move water from their roots, up through their stems, into their leaves, and out into the air.

YOUR TURN TO EXPERIMENT

❄ **CELERY** can also change color through capillary action. Design an experiment with water and food coloring to see for yourself.

❄ Draw your experiment idea below:

SNOW GOLEM SHOOTER

Shooting projectiles and investigating force.

A snow golem, despite his scary appearance, can defend a player against hostile mobs by **THROWING** snowballs at enemies. He must be created by a player or randomly created by an Enderman. He moves around by sliding on a snow path he creates for himself. He can also supply **SNOWBALLS** on demand for players building igloos. In this activity, you'll create a snow golem that demonstrates how we can use **FORCE** to shoot pom-pom "snowballs" from pool noodles.

INSTRUCTIONS

1. Have a parent use the knife to cut the pool noodles into the following sizes:
   - One 3-inch piece of orange pool noodle
   - One 3-inch piece of white pool noodle
   - One 2-inch piece of white pool noodle

2. Use the scissors to cut about an inch off the open end of the balloon. Set aside.

2. Pull the open end of the balloon over the end of the 3-inch white noodle so that it fits snuggly and blocks the noodle hole on one side.

3. Snap two toothpicks in half to make four halves.

4. Stack the white noodle pieces so that the 2-inch white noodle is on the bottom and the open holes face forward and noodle ends are flush with each other. Use the toothpick halves to spear the two white noodle pieces together. (Add more toothpicks as needed.)

5. Set the orange noodle piece on the table with a hole pointing up and use the marker to draw a pumpkin face on one side. Draw buttons on the white noodles.

6. Using the other toothpick halves, join the pumpkin face to the larger white noodle piece so that the balloon extends out from the golem's back.

7. Use the 2 whole toothpicks as arms

for the snow golem.

8. Stick the unused portion of balloon out of the top of the snow golem's head for a pumpkin stem decoration.

9. Insert a marshmallow (or other projectile) in the front of the center noodle. Pinch the balloon, pull it back gently, and let it go. A marshmallow should shoot out of your snow golem.

WHAT REALLY HAPPENED?

☼ A force is a push or a pull on an object. The force you use to pull back the balloon will be transferred to the snowball. Pulling it back farther will create a greater force than pulling it back only partway.

YOUR TURN TO EXPERIMENT

☼ What other objects can you shoot out of your snow golem? Which ones travel the greatest distance?

☼ Make targets for your snowballs and have a competition with a friend.

MATERIALS

- serrated knife
- 2 pool noodles of different colors (orange and white)
- 1 (white) balloon
- scissors
- 4–6 toothpicks
- black permanent marker
- mini marshmallows or small white or silver pom-poms (they should fit inside the hole of the pool noodle)

Torches are found in dark areas around Minecraft, providing light for the player. Here, make your own torch by turning milk into plastic and adding the ink from a highlighter to make it fluorescent (you will need a black light to see the fluorescence).

INSTRUCTIONS

1. Measure 1 cup of milk in a glass measuring cup. Microwave for 2 minutes. Have a parent help you remove the milk from the microwave: it will be hot.

2. In a separate bowl, measure 4 teaspoons of white vinegar and add 5–7 drops of food coloring.

3. Have an adult remove the ink from the highlighter and add it to the bowl containing the vinegar and food coloring.

4. Add the colored vinegar to the hot milk.

5. Stir with the spoon. The milk will curdle and form clumps.

6. Strain the milk through the cloth, collecting the clumps in the cloth. Discard the liquid.

7. Use the rubber band to turn the fabric into a pouch containing the milk clumps. Allow to cool for 20–30 minutes. This is your milk plastic.

8. While you wait, use the black marker to color the whole outside of the toilet paper roll.

8. When the milk plastic is cool enough to handle, unwrap the clumps and smush them together into the shape of a ball. Allow the ball to harden for 30–60 minutes.

9. Place the milk plastic ball on top of the toilet paper roll. After the milk plastic has completely dried and hardened (2–3 days), ask a grown-up to hot glue it to the toilet paper roll.

10. In a dark room lit with the black light, check out your torch.

WHAT REALLY HAPPENED?

☀ Black lights emit ultraviolet (UV) light, which we cannot see. Fluorescence is light given off by certain substances (like highlighter ink) when they absorb UV light. First the substance absorbs energy, and then it gives off light. The torch emits light thanks to its fluorescent highlighter ink.

YOUR TURN TO EXPERIMENT

☀ There are some animals that naturally fluoresce. Do some research to see which animals have the ability of biofluorescence and how this adaptation helps them survive in their habitat.

TIME

1 hour and 20 minutes (plus 2–3 days of hardening time)

MATERIALS

◆ 1 cup whole milk
◆ glass measuring cup
◆ small bowl
◆ 4 teaspoons of white vinegar
◆ yellow food coloring
◆ orange or yellow highlighter with liquid ink
◆ scrap of fabric or cheesecloth
◆ rubber band
◆ empty toilet paper roll
◆ black permanent marker
◆ black light
◆ hot glue gun

TALL TOWER ENGINEERING

Think like an engineer and build a tower that's tall *and strong!*

Minecraft is the perfect place to fine-tune your tower-building skills, but you are limited to **BUILDING STRUCTURES** that are 255 blocks high. In this activity, the only limits are based in **PHYSICS**. Experiment with different bases and shapes and think like an engineer to make a marshmallow skyscraper that's **STRONG AND STURDY** enough to last!

INSTRUCTIONS:

1. Consider your strategy. Before you begin building, figure out which shapes you can make with toothpicks and marshmallows. Which one will make the strongest base? (Wobble them to find out.)

2. Using what you learned about the strengths of the shapes, build the tallest, free-standing (not touching anything) tower you can imagine. Use the cutting board or cookie sheet for a solid foundation.

3. Measure your tower and record the height below.

DATA

Make a sketch of your designs below, measure and record the height of each.

Trial 1:	Trial 2:
Height:	Height:

TIME

30 minutes

MATERIALS

- bag of miniature marshmallows (leave open overnight so they're stale)
- box of at least 100 toothpicks
- cutting board or cookie sheet
- tape measure, ruler or meter/yardstick

WHAT REALLY HAPPENED?

※ An engineer is a person who designs and builds complex machines and structures. The process you used to create your tall tower is very similar to the way engineers think about problems and design solutions. This method of problem-solving is called the **ENGINEERING DESIGN PROCESS.**

※ Different shapes have different strengths. Triangles make a strong base, which is why they are often used by builders.

YOUR TURN TO EXPERIMENT

※ Do some research to find out which shapes engineers use to build really tall towers and really long bridges. Find photos of famous tall buildings online and see if you can copy the design with marshmallows and toothpicks.

※ Challenge your parents, siblings, or friends to build a tower taller than yours. Who can build the tallest free-standing tower with marshmallows and toothpicks?

BIOME ENGINEERING
Build a biome and watch it grow.

biome is an **ECOLOGICAL COMMUNITY,** like a rainforest, desert, or grassland. The natural world has a total of fourteen biomes (five aquatic and nine land biomes). There are sixty-two different biomes in Minecraft. Try building your own biome—either based in **NATURE** or similar to one in Minecraft. You could even come up with your very own biome and give it a name!

INSTRUCTIONS

1. Place a 1-inch layer of gravel on the bottom of the container.

2. Place a 1-inch layer of sand over the gravel.

3. Mix 2 cups of soil and 1 cup of sand. Place a 2–3 inch layer of the sand/soil mixture over the gravel. (For desert biomes, mix ½ cup of soil with 3 cups of sand.)

4. Plant the plants in the soil. (If using seeds, allow time for them to sprout.)

5. Add small critters, if you choose.

6. Gently add water until you see a small amount of water in the bottom of the tank.

7. Place the biome in a sunny location and add water when needed.

WHAT REALLY HAPPENED?

❋ Biomes are large geographical areas with specific climates, plants and animals.

❋ The biosphere is the part of the Earth's atmosphere that supports life. It includes both living and nonliving things.

❋ Engineers call artificial environments (ones made by people) biodomes. A biodome is a model that is designed to represent a particular environment and the organisms that live there. You created one!

TIME

1 hour

MATERIALS

- container such as a plastic aquarium, bottom half of a soda bottle, terrarium, or clear candy jar

- substrate: aquarium gravel/ rocks, sand, and soil

- plants or seeds, succulents, or cacti

- small critters, such as worms, snails, or slugs (optional)

YOUR TURN TO EXPERIMENT

❋ Experiment with your biome. Change the amounts of substrate or the depth of the layers. Make a few different biomes and change the amount of light and water they get. What are the best conditions for your biome?

❋ Try making a self-sufficient environment by putting a lid on your biome. If it succeeds, you won't need to water your biome because the water will recycle itself. You will be able to watch the water cycle in action!

❋ Design a new biome! Research to find out which plants and animals can live together.

CHARGED CREEPER

Repurpose and rewire a motor.

Creepers are scary enough to begin with, but **CHARGED CREEPERS** are even more deadly! Charged by a lightning strike, this kind of creeper has a glowing blue aura and twice the **EXPLOSIVE POWER.** You can make your own charged creeper by upcycling a vibrating toothbrush motor and retrofitting it with a new battery. **WATCH IT GO!**

INSTRUCTIONS

1. With help from a grown-up, break open the toothbrush and remove the motor and battery. You may need to use pliers. Be careful not to damage the wires.

2. Observe how the motor works by turning the switch on and off. Experiment with the circuit by taking wires on and off the ends of the battery and switching them around to understand how they work.

3. Remove the old battery and insert the watch battery. You may need to use electrical tape to keep the metal ends of the wires attached to the smaller battery. You can also use aluminum foil to close any gaps that may have formed.

4. Cut a small section out of one end of the pool noodle as needed so that the motor and battery can be placed inside. Use clear packing tape to keep the battery tucked up inside the pool noodle with the motor sticking out of the noodle.

5. Use the permanent marker to draw a creeper on the pool noodle. (The head should be at the end opposite the battery.)

6. Turn on the motor, sit the creeper up with the motor on the table or floor, and watch your charged creeper vibrate across the surface.

MATERIALS

- vibrating toothbrush (used or new)
- pliers
- watch battery (3-volt battery)
- electrical tape
- aluminum foil
- 4 inches of green pool noodle
- clear packing tape
- black permanent marker
- knife

WHAT REALLY HAPPENED?

※ A circuit is a path that allows electricity to flow. Materials that allow electric current to pass through them easily are called conductors. Conductors can be used to link the positive and negative ends of a battery, forming a circuit.

※ If you experimented with the wires on the battery, you noticed that the battery had to be connected at the positive end and the negative end. If one end is not connected, energy cannot flow and power the device.

YOUR TURN TO EXPERIMENT

What other inventions could you make from a toothbrush motor and battery?

Have a charged **CREEPER DANCE PARTY.** Invite some friends to make charged creepers with you and allow them to dance around on the floor together. Is there any way to control which way the charged creepers move?

STEM QUEST
MATH MINUTE II

These problems use wordplay instead of swordplay.

Minecrafters love to joke around and have fun. Have you heard these jokes? Find the solution to the math problems at right and then use the key below to fill in the punch lines.

KEY

A	B	C	D	E	F
2	9	16	12	5	11

G	H	I	J	K	L
20	19	26	23	13	8

M	N	O	P	Q	R
6	18	10	4	3	15

S	T	U	V	W	X
21	7	17	1	25	22

Y	Z				
24	14				

1. WHAT IS A CREEPER'S FAVORITE COLOR?

4 +5	4 +4	2 +3	21 +4
Letter			

2. WHAT IS A WITCH'S FAVORITE SUBJECT IN SCHOOL?

15 +6	1 +3	0 +5	1 +7	3 +5	18 +8	11 +7	3 +17
Letter							

DIG IN
Mine for resources like a pro!

As any Minecrafter knows, mining is essential to surviving the game. Players have to dig into their world's **NATURAL RESOURCES** to gather different types of **STONE, METALS, WOOD, AND ORE.** Without these materials, players cannot build or create structures. In the real world, mining for resources is a difficult task. Resources have to be located, **EXTRACTED FROM THE EARTH** without damaging the landscape, and then changed to new forms to be useful. See if you're up for the challenge of a real miner in this dig-and-discover activity.

INSTRUCTIONS

1. Ask a friend or parent to fill the bottom of the container with one color of craft sand. Add several resources to the sand. Add a second layer of sand in a contrasting color and then add the remaining resources. Top with the third layer of sand to hide all the resources.

2. Observe the layers of sand by looking at the side of the container. The layers of sand represent the layers of soil and rock in the earth. Your goal is to remove the resources while not disturbing the layers of sand.

3. Use colored pencils, crayons, or markers to draw the layers of sand in the top box at right.

5. Ask a friend to set the stopwatch for 60 seconds, which will represent one day of mining.

6. When your friend says go, you will have 60 seconds to very carefully remove as many resources as possible using your tools. Remember, your goal is to remove the resources with as little change as possible to the sand layers.

7. After your 60-second "day", record the number of resources you found on the table on page 56.

8. Repeat Steps 3–5 until all the resources have been mined.

9. Draw the layers of sand in the bottom box at right after you finish mining.

LAYERS BEFORE MINING:

LAYERS AFTER MINING:

MATERIALS

- plastic, transparent, shoebox-sized container

- 3 colors of craft sand in contrasting colors

- 30 "resources" such as coins, rocks, balled-up aluminum foil, crystals, etc.

- "tools" such as skewers, spoons, toothpicks, tweezers, forks, straws, etc.

- colored pencils, markers, or crayons

- stopwatch or timer

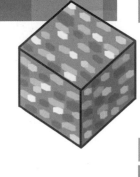

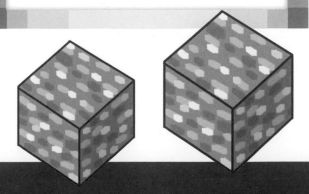

RECORD THE NUMBER OF RESOURCES YOU MINED EACH DAY:

Time	Number of Resources
Day 1	
Day 2	
Day 3	
Day 4	
Day 5	
Day 6	
Day 7	

WHAT REALLY HAPPENED?

❉ Miners dig into the Earth to remove natural resources. Natural resources are items that we can use, such as coal or gold.

❉ Earth has lots of resources, but it takes a long time for them to form. Just like in this activity, as more and more resources are removed by mining, it becomes harder to find more of the same.

❉ Mining can be disruptive to the environment. Land must be cleared, but digging into the Earth can disrupt plants and animals that live there.

❉ Scientists are looking for new ways to remove resources to protect the environment. They are also looking for new ways to make things that will require less mining. Do you have any ideas?

YOUR TURN TO EXPERIMENT

Draw or create a brand new machine or tool that will help find resources and protect the soil.

MINECART MOTION
Convert potential energy to kinetic energy

Minecarts are wonderful tools. Not only can you use them to move your resources, but you can also take a ride in them—for **TRANSPORTATION** or fun. One way that minecarts are **POWERED** is by gravity. Here you will create your own model of a minecart and design a track for it while learning how **SIMPLE MACHINES** help us get things done.

INSTRUCTIONS FOR MINECART

1. Color the inner box of the matchbox with dark markers to make it look like a minecart.

2. Cut a straw into two pieces that are slightly shorter than the width of the long sides of the matchbox.

3. Turn the matchbox upside down so that the open part of the box is touching the table.

4. Tape the straw pieces to the bottom of the matchbox, parallel to and closest to the short sides of the box. These will be hold the axles for your wheels.

5. Fill the middle of each bobbin (or wheel) with a piece of molding clay.

6. Insert the toothpicks into the straws that are attached to the matchbox.

7. Push the bobbins onto the ends of the toothpicks.

8. Turn the cart over and see if your cart rolls. Make adjustments until your cart can easily be pushed or rolled down a ramp.

INSTRUCTIONS FOR RAMP

1. Use different lengths of straws to make vertical supports for your ramp. You will need two pieces of equal length for each section.

2. Attach the straw pieces to the foam board using molding clay.

3. Rip off a long piece of aluminum foil that is the length of your foam board.

TIME
30 minutes

MATERIALS
◆ small, empty matchbox
◆ gray and/or black markers
◆ 12–14 straight straws
◆ scissors
◆ clear tape
◆ 4 sewing bobbins
◆ molding clay
◆ 2 round toothpicks
◆ aluminum foil
◆ foam board

4. Fold the foil in half lengthwise. Then fold up the edges to make guard rails for the ramp.

5. Use tape to attach the ramp to the tops of the straws.

6. Try putting your minecart at the top of the ramp and letting it roll to the bottom. Did it work? If not, make adjustments to the track or to the minecart.

WHAT REALLY HAPPENED?

✳ Simple machines are machines we use every day to make work easier. The simple machine in this activity is a wheel and axle. The bobbins are the wheels, and the toothpicks are the axles. The wheels and axles allowed the minecart to roll along the tracks.

✳ The track you created is another simple machine called an inclined plane. An inclined plane is a ramp that lets you transport items quickly from one place to another.

YOUR TURN TO EXPERIMENT

✳ Place small objects in the minecart and observe how they change the cart's speed. Does it go faster or slower?

AWKWARD POTION

Learn about density with this potion that just wont mix

Awkward potions in Minecraft are base potions with no effects. They are **COMBINED** with other ingredients to create useful potions. Where do you think Awkward potion got its name? The potion in this activity is a bit awkward, too: The ingredients will not combine. When added carefully, you will be able to see ingredients with different densities form **SEPARATE LAYERS.** And since there are no chemical reactions to worry about with these ingredients, you can be very creative and make your own **PATTERN** of layers.

INSTRUCTIONS

1. The quantities of ingredients in this potion can be varied based on which ingredients you have available at home or the size of your container. As a general rule, add ¼–½ cup of liquids for each ingredient.

2. Do not mix or shake the potion at any time during the activity. Only mix solutions before adding them to the glass. If your potion becomes mixed accidentally, allow it to sit for several hours or overnight to see the layers.

3. Add honey to your glass container.

4. In a separate dish, mix corn syrup with a few squirts of food coloring.

5. Pour the corn syrup and food coloring mixture into the container, on top of the honey. (If the opening to your glass or jar is narrow, use a funnel.)

6. Add glitter glue to your container, on top of the corn syrup mixture.

7. Add dish soap to your container, on top of the glitter glue.

8. Pour milk into a clean container. Add powered watercolor or food coloring. Stir to combine.

TIME

20 minutes to make
(30–45 minutes to
settle)

MATERIALS

- honey
- glass or jar
- corn syrup
- food coloring
- glitter paint or glue
- dish soap
- milk (skim)
- powdered watercolor (optional)
- tonic water
- glitter (optional)
- vegetable oil
- baby oil
- small bowls for mixing
- green olives stuffed with red peppers (optional)
- small Styrofoam balls (optional)
- funnel (optional)

9. Pour the colored milk on top of the dish soap.

10. Pour tonic water into a clean bowl and add glitter. Stir to combine.

11. Pour the tonic water on top of the milk mixture.

12. Pour the vegetable oil into a clean bowl. Add several squirts of food coloring. Stir to combine.

13. Carefully pour the vegetable oil mixture into the container, on top of the tonic water.

14. Pour the baby oil into a clean bowl. Add glitter. Stir to combine.

15. Carefully pour the baby oil and glitter mixture into the glass.

16. It would be fun to add a fermented spider eye, wouldn't it? Use filled olives or Styrofoam peanuts instead, turning your Awkward potion into a potion of Weakness.

17. Let the potion settle for 30–45 minutes.

WHAT REALLY HAPPENED?

✳ Did you notice the layers created in this potion? Each layer is "awkward" because it does not mix with the others.

✳ The reason the layers did not mix is that they have different densities. **DENSITY** measures how tightly packed an object's particles are. When you combine liquids of different densities, they naturally separate. The liquids that are less dense float. The liquids that are denser sink.

✳ If you used whole milk, you may have noticed the milk mixing with the dish soap. That's because the fat in the milk allowed it to combine with the soap. If you used fat-free milk, the milk should have stayed on top of the dish soap.

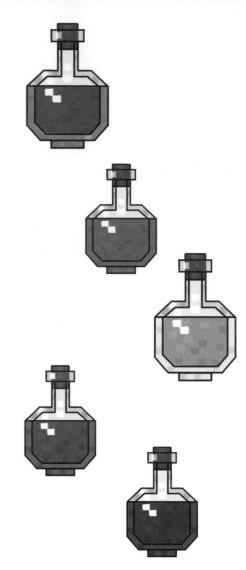

YOUR TURN TO EXPERIMENT

What would happen if you added other common liquid ingredients to your mixture? Try it and find out!

STEM QUEST NOTES:

ANSWER KEY

STEM Quest Math Minute, Page 32

TNT
5 gunpowder
+ 4 blocks of sand
_____
9 items total

Bow
3 sticks
+ 3 pieces of string
_____
6 items total

Arrows
1 stick
1 feather
+ 1 flint
_____
3 items total

Enchantment Table
4 obsidian blocks
2 diamonds
+ 1 book
_____
7 items total

Bed
3 blocks of wool
+ 3 planks
_____
6 items total

Wood Pickaxe
2 sticks
+ 3 wood planks
_____
5 items total

1. sticks
2. Arrow recipe

STEM Quest Math Minute, Page 52

1. What is Creeper's favorite color?

	4 +5	4 +4	2 +3	21 +4
Answer	9	8	6	25
Letter	B	L	E	W

2. What is a witch's favorite subject in school?

	15 +6	1 +3	0 +5	1 +7	3 +5	18 +8	11 +7	3 +17
Answer	21	4	5	8	8	26	18	20
Letter	S	P	E	L	L	I	N	G